The
World's Best
Holiday
Jokes

In this series:

The World's Best Dirty Jokes
More of the World's Best Dirty Jokes
Still More of the World's Best Dirty Jokes
The World's Best Irish Jokes
More of the World's Best Irish Jokes
The World's Best Jewish Jokes
More of the World's Best Jewish Jokes
The World's Best Doctor Jokes
More of the World's Best Doctor Jokes
The World's Best Dirty Stories
The World's Best Dirty Limericks
The World's Best Dirty Songs
The World's Best Aussie Jokes
The World's Best Catholic Jokes
The World's Best Mother-In-Law Jokes
The World's Best Russian Jokes
The World's Best Fishing Jokes
The World's Best Salesman Jokes
The World's Best Computer Jokes
The World's Best Scottish Jokes
The World's Best Cricket Jokes
The World's Best Golf Jokes
The World's Best Maggie Thatcher Jokes
The World's Best Lawyer Jokes
The World's Best Business Jokes
The World's Best Holiday Jokes
The World's Best Acting Jokes

The World's Best Holiday Jokes

Edward Phillips

Illustrated by Tony Blundell

ANGUS & ROBERTSON PUBLISHERS

ANGUS & ROBERTSON PUBLISHERS

16 Golden Square, London W1R 4BN,
United Kingdom and
Unit 4, Eden Park, 31 Waterloo Road,
North Ryde, NSW, Australia 2113.

First published in the United Kingdom by
Angus & Robertson (UK) in 1989
First published in Australia by
Angus & Robertson Publishers in 1989
Reprinted 1990

Text copyright © Edward Phillips 1989
Illustrations copyright © Tony Blundell 1989

British Library Cataloguing in Publication Data
Phillips, Edward
    The world's best holiday jokes
    I. Title
    828'.91402

ISBN 0 207 16468 1

Typeset in Great Britain by Poole Typesetting (Wessex) Limited, Bournemouth
Printed and bound in Great Britain by
BPCC Hazell Books, Aylesbury
Member of BPCC Ltd.

At a small seaside hotel, a young lady on holiday was sunning herself on the flat roof, clad only in a tiny bikini. Deciding that she might as well get an all-over tan, she glanced round to make sure that the roof was not overlooked and then removed her bikini. As she lay there on her stomach, the hotel manager suddenly appeared and said, 'We don't allow nude sunbathing up here, miss!'

Hastily grabbing a beach robe, the young lady said, 'But surely no one can see me up here!'

'That's what you think,' said the manager. 'You're lying on the skylight over the dining room!'

A couple of young holidaymakers were canoodling under the pier. 'Darling, you're one in a million,' the young man murmured.

'So are your chances,' replied the young lady sharply.

Two men on holiday in Wales were driving home when their car broke down on a lonely country road. There was just one isolated farmhouse to be seen and they trudged across the fields and knocked on the door. It was opened by a very attractive woman in her thirties who told them that they would not be able to get their car repaired until the following morning. It turned out that her husband had recently died and she now lived all alone on the farm. She offered them dinner and a bed for the night. The two friends accepted gratefully.

A couple of months later, one of the two men received an official-looking letter. That night in the pub, he met his holiday companion and said, 'Henry, do you remember the night our car broke down when we were coming back from Wales? And the farmhouse we stayed at? And that attractive widow?'

'Yes, I do,' said Henry, a little nervously.

'Did you, by any chance, spend a little time that night in her bedroom?'

'Well, yes,' muttered Henry.

'And did you, by any chance, give her my name and address?'

'Yes, I did,' admitted Henry. 'But it was only a joke. I didn't think you'd get upset about it.'

'Oh, I'm not upset,' said his friend. 'It's just that I received a letter from her solicitors this morning. It seems she died last week and left me the farmhouse and three thousand acres.'

An American on holiday in England visited the British Museum and was intrigued by a magnificent Egyptian mummy. 'How old is this exhibit?' he asked a guide.

'Four thousand years and three months, sir,' said the guide.

'How can you be so exact about the age of a thing like that?' demanded the American.

'Well, sir,' replied the guide, 'the gentleman who donated it to the Museum said it was four thousand years old, and that was exactly three months ago.'

A lady went on a package tour of Europe which visited twenty-five countries in seven days. One day she found she'd missed four countries. She didn't have a window seat.

A party of German holidaymakers was being taken on a coach tour through the English countryside. With Teutonic thoroughness, they checked their watches at each stop and complained bitterly if they were so much as one minute behind schedule. When the coach pulled up at one historic site, the guide announced, 'Ladies and gentlemen, this is Runnymede. Under that historic oak tree over there, the famous Magna Carta was signed.'

'Ven did zis take place?' asked one of the Germans.

'1215,' replied the guide.

With a glance at his watch, the German exclaimed, 'So! Ve haf missed it by seven minutes!'

A holidaymaker in Paris was dining in a restaurant when he noticed a fly in his soup. He summoned the waiter and, being proud of his knowledge of the French language, pointed to his plate and said, '*Le mouche!*'

The waiter glanced at the plate and replied, '*Non, Monsieur – c'est* la *mouche.*'

'Good Lord!' exclaimed the diner. 'You French certainly have first-class eyesight!'

A husband and wife bound for a holiday in Majorca were waiting patiently in the airport lounge. Suddenly the husband said, 'You know, darling, I wish we'd brought the piano with us.'

'Don't be ridiculous!' exclaimed his wife. 'Why on earth should we have brought the piano?'

'Because I've left our tickets on top of it,' replied the husband.

The charter flight to Tangier had just taken off and the captain made his usual speech of welcome over the intercom. Then, forgetting that he had not switched off his microphone, and that all the passengers could still hear him, he turned to his co-pilot and said, 'Take over for a bit, Bob – I'm so tired that all I'd like to do now is have a pint of beer and a quiet, relaxing session with that new blonde flight hostess!'

Back in the passenger cabin, the flight hostess blushed bright crimson and rushed down the aisle towards the cabin to warn the captain that his microphone was still switched on. One of the holidaymakers, a dear old lady, said sweetly, 'There's no need to rush, my dear – he won't have finished his beer yet.'

A rather large and overbearing woman walked into a travel bureau with her meek-looking husband in tow. 'We would like two bookings on a luxury cruise,' she said loudly.

'Certainly, madam,' said the booking clerk. 'Have you any particular requirements?'

'Yes,' muttered the husband. 'Book us on separate ships.'

A furniture manufacturer from the North Country decided to take a short holiday in Paris. After a few days spent visiting furniture shops and exhibitions, he was sitting one lunchtime at a table outside a pavement café when a very attractive young lady sat down in the vacant chair opposite him. The man could hardly believe his luck, but it soon became apparent that the young lady spoke no English; and his French being non-existent, it seemed that nothing would come of the encounter.

Then suddenly the girl turned the menu over and drew a picture of a bottle of wine and two glasses on the back. The manufacturer got the idea at once and summoned a waiter.

When the wine arrived, the young lady drew a picture of a plate and a knife and fork on the menu, and the manufacturer

promptly ordered dinner for two. After a truly splendid meal, the girl sketched a picture of a large double bed on the menu.

The manufacturer looked at her in amazement. 'By 'eck!' he exclaimed, 'that's amazing! How did you know I was in the furniture business?'

A family on holiday in the South of England paid a visit to Beachy Head. Mother and the kids sat on the cliff-top admiring the view. Father, carrying the haversack with all their picnic things, walked to the cliff edge and peered down at the sea raging hundreds of feet below. Little Johnny walked cautiously over to him and said, 'Dad – Mum says will you keep further away from the edge or else give me the sandwiches.'

Two Scotsmen came down to London for a week's holiday. On their first night, they walked into a very swanky restaurant in Mayfair. When the waiter came over to their table, one of them said, 'We only have £5 to spend. What do you suggest?'

The waiter looked at them for a moment and then said, 'Another restaurant.'

'**I** shall always remember the day we first set eyes on the Grand Canyon. My husband's face dropped a mile.'

'You mean he wasn't impressed?'

'No. I mean he fell over the edge.'

Two young holidaymakers were sitting on the beach gazing out to sea. 'You know, Bill,' said the girl, 'you remind me of the sea.'

'Really?' said the young man. 'You mean I'm wild and romantic?'

'No. I mean you make me sick.'

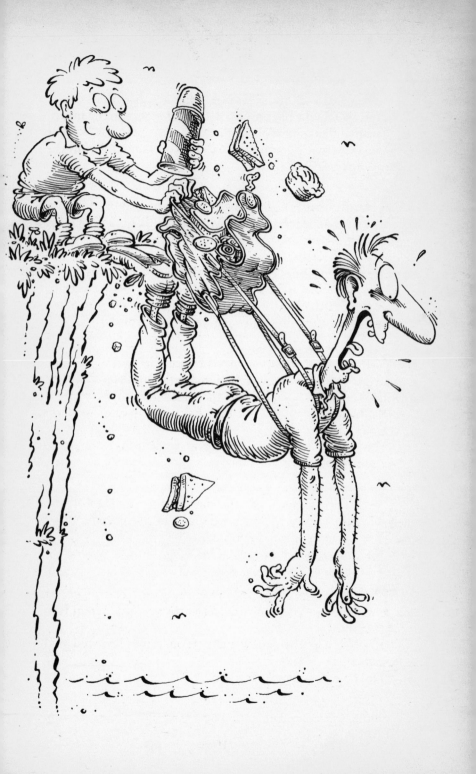

An Englishman was on holiday in Ireland. Feeling thirsty, he walked into a public house. There was no one there but a barmaid, polishing glasses. 'I'm sorry, sir,' she said, 'but I can't serve you. We don't open for another hour. You're welcome to sit in here and wait.'

'Thank you very much,' said the Englishman. He sat down in a corner and opened his newspaper.

A few minutes later, the barmaid came across to him and said, 'Would you like a drink while you're waiting, sir?'

A young man on a motoring holiday in the country was driving his car down a very narrow lane. There was a concealed bend ahead and, as he approached, another car with a large woman at the wheel shot round it on the wrong side of the road. The young man swerved on to the grass verge, and as the other car hurtled past the woman stuck her head out of the window and shouted, 'Pig!'

Shocked, he yelled 'Cow!' at the top of his voice and drove on.

Rounding the bend, he ran smack into the biggest pig he had ever seen in his life.

Most people go on holiday to forget things. And when they arrive and open their cases, they find out just how much they've forgotten.

Frank decided to spend his holiday at the annual beer festival in Munich. On the first evening, he struck up an acquaintance with Ilsa, a charming young lady who very kindly invited him home with her to spend the night. The next morning, he was just about to leave when Ilsa said, 'Herr Frank – haven't you forgotten something?'

'Pardon?' said Frank.

'You know,' said Ilsa. 'Isn't there something you have to give me?'

'Is there?' said Frank, puzzled.

'*Mein Gott!*' screamed Ilsa. 'My marks, my marks!'

'Oh, sorry,' said Frank. 'Eight out of ten.'

An old Irishman had been on holiday in Lourdes. On his return home, he was stopped by the customs officer at the airport and asked to open his suitcase. The customs man pulled out a bottle and asked, 'Now then, sir, what's in this?'

'Holy water,' said the Irishman. 'It's just holy water from the shrine at Lourdes.'

The customs officer pulled out the cork and took a sniff. 'This isn't holy water!' he exclaimed. 'It's brandy!'

'Glory be to God!' exclaimed the old Irishman. 'It's a miracle!'

Jim and Janet were spending their annual holiday motoring through the Lake District. At the top of a steep hill just outside a small village, their car broke down. Jim got out and crawled under the car to see if he could locate the trouble. After about ten minutes, Janet became impatient and crawled under the car to help him. The minutes ticked by and the two of them, in close proximity under the car, forgot all about the job in hand and turned their attention to amatory matters.

After about half an hour, locked in a passionate embrace, they were startled to hear an authoritative voice demanding what they were up to. They glanced up to see the village policeman and half the local inhabitants glaring at them.

'Oh!' said Jim. 'We were – er – trying to fix the transmission.'

'Well, while you're down there, you'd better fix your brakes too,' said the constable. 'Your car rolled down the hill ten minutes ago.'

An unmarried middle-aged lady booked into a hotel in Brighton for a week's holiday. Shortly after she had been shown up to her room, she rang down and demanded that the manager come up immediately. When he arrived, she said indignantly, 'It's disgraceful! I looked out of my window and there, in the room across the way, is a man taking a bath – completely naked!'

The manager looked out and said, 'But, madam, that window is quite high – I can only see the top of the man's head.'

'Oh, yes?' said the lady. 'You just stand on this chair!'

Two passengers on a train bound for London struck up a conversation and discovered that they were both going on holiday. The journey was interminable, with frequent unscheduled stops and long waits at stations. Finally, many hours later, and very late, the train arrived at its destination. One of the two men breathed a sigh of relief. 'Well!' he said. 'That's the worst part of the journey over!'

'Where are you bound for?' asked his companion.

'Hong Kong,' he replied.

Two friends were bound for a holiday in the Mediterranean. One of them looked out of the cabin window of the aeroplane and exclaimed, 'Good Lord! Look at all those people down there! They look just like ants!'

His friend peered over his shoulder and said, 'They *are* ants. We haven't taken off yet.'

A motorist on holiday in the West Country stopped his car and asked a local farmer, 'Could you tell me how far it is to Exeter?'

'Well,' said the farmer, scratching his head, 'it's about 24,997 miles in the direction you're going, and about three if you turn round and go the other way.'

In a holiday hotel on the South Coast, a large notice proclaimed: 'Please do not insult our waiters by tipping.' Close by was a small box, placed there by the waiters themselves. It was marked: 'Insults'.

A woman on a holiday trip to the New Forest stood in awe in front of an enormous tree. 'Oh, marvellous and ancient oak!' she enthused. 'If you could only speak, what would you say?'

'Well,' said the tour guide, 'it would probably say, 'Pardon me, madam, but I'm an elm.'

If you are going on holiday abroad and are thinking of learning one or two useful phrases in the local language, there is one you should be sure to memorize: 'You forgot my change!'

A young man on vacation in France was travelling by train from Paris to Lyon. The train made an unscheduled stop and, thinking that they had arrived at the station, he gathered up his luggage, threw open the door and jumped out. As he disappeared down the embankment in a flurry of arms and legs, the guard, who was watching from his window, muttered, 'C'est magnifique, mais ce n'est pas la gare!'

Sign in a French holiday hotel: 'Guests which may entertain any desires during the night are advised to ring for the chambermaid.'

'Where did you stay in Boulogne?'
'At the Hotel George V.'
'But the Hotel George V is in Paris!'
'Is it? No wonder it was such a long walk to the beach!'

'And what do you think of our Switzerland, monsieur? A beautiful country, is it not?'
'Oh, I don't know. Take away your mountains and your valleys and your lakes, and what have you got?'

A motorist on holiday in London parked his car in a prohibited zone. A policeman strolled over and said, 'You can't park here, you know.'
'Why not?' said the motorist. That sign says "Fine For Parking".'

A tourist visiting Mexico noticed one of the natives dozing in the shade of a large tree. As it was the middle of a weekday morning, he said, 'Don't you have a job?'

'No,' said the Mexican.

'Well, why don't you get yourself one instead of lazing about all day?'

'What for?'

'So that you can earn some money," said the tourist.

'Why should I want to do that?' asked the local.

'So you could improve your standard of living. Then you could start saving.'

'What for?'

'Well, when you'd saved enough, you could retire and then you'd be able to take it easy and relax.'

'That's just what I'm doing now,' said the Mexican, and promptly went back to sleep.

He: 'Did you manage to pick up any Italian when you were in Venice?'
She: 'Yes, I did.'
He: 'Let's hear some then.'
She: 'He spoke English.'

A holidaymaker motoring to Wales arrived at the Severn Bridge in his very ancient and dilapidated old bone-shaker. The attendant stuck his head out of the toll-booth, glanced at the vehicle and said, '£5 for the car, sir.'

'Sold!' said the motorist.

A fisherman on holiday in Ireland hired a local boatman to take him down the Liffey. 'You're sure you know this river?' he asked anxiously as the boat moved rapidly along with the swift-flowing current.

'Sure, I know this river like the back of me hand, sir!' said the boatman. 'I know every bend and current. And I know every rock in it, large and small!'

At that moment, the boat struck a submerged rock and shuddered violently. 'You see, sir!' cried the boatman. 'There's one of them now!'

Holiday visitor to Norfolk: 'When I stayed here last year, there were two windmills. What happened to the other one?'

Local farmer: 'There was only enough wind for one so we took it down.'

One of the attractions of the holiday resort was a ride in an aeroplane, a decrepit and none-too-safe pre-war biplane. A dear old lady who had never flown before decided to give it a go. She paid her £25 for the fifteen-minute flight and the pilot thought he would give her a treat. He put the plane through its whole repertoire, diving, spinning, turning, twisting and looping the loop. When they finally landed, the old lady, pale as a sheet, gasped, 'Thank you for both of those rides, young man!'

'Both?' said the pilot. 'There was only one.'

'I make it two,' said the old lady. 'My first and my last.'

When vacation time came round, George decided to be really adventurous and visit America. His itinerary included a visit to an Indian reservation in Colorado. As he wandered around, he noticed an Indian riding a pony with his squaw trudging behind him carrying an enormous bundle. Indignantly, he said, 'Look here, why doesn't the squaw ride?'

With a look of surprise, the Indian said, 'She got no pony!'

On a cruise to the West Indies, the husband was seasick every day. On the sixth day out his wife asked solicitously, 'Are you going to try a little dinner tonight, dear?'

'No thanks,' he replied. 'Just chuck it straight over the side and save me the trouble.'

'How did you enjoy your holiday on the Continent?' a little girl was asked.

'It was very nice,' she replied, 'but I did get tired of being interested in everything.'

Two holidaymakers fell into conversation on the train to Worthing. 'Have you been here before?' asked one.

'Oh, yes,' replied the other. 'I come here every year.'

'What hotel would you recommend?'

'Try the Imperial.'

'Have you always stayed there?'

'No, never – but I've stayed at all the others.'

Don't go to Brighton for your holidays. Last year a little boy went down to the beach and he built a sandcastle. Ten minutes later, an attendant walked up and handed him a rates demand.

Two Scottish businessmen on a skiing holiday in Switzerland went out alone one morning, and due to their inexperience shot over the edge of a 100-foot drop. Luckily they landed in thick snow and their injuries were slight, but they were unable to move, and there was nothing for it but to wait until help arrived. They lay there for several hours and then heard the rescue party approaching. A voice shouted, 'Hello! We're from the Red Cross!'

Hurriedly, one of the Scotsmen shouted back, 'We already gave at the office!'

A holiday visitor to London went into the Royal Academy of Arts Summer Exhibition. One of the attendants was standing beside a large, elaborate gilt frame. The visitor looked at it in disgust and sneered, 'I suppose this is a typical example of so-called modern art!'

'No, sir,' said the attendant. 'Actually, it's a mirror.'

In the dining room of a large seaside hotel a waiter spilled a plate of soup over the jacket of a visiting holidaymaker. The waiter seemed quite unconcerned, but the manager rushed up and said, 'A thousand apologies, sir! Let me take your jacket – I'll have it sponged and cleaned immediately.' The guest, somewhat placated, removed his jacket, and the manager hurried off with it.

The waiter, who had been watching the proceedings with a scowl on his face, tapped the holidaymaker on the shoulder and said, 'Oy! You're not allowed in the dining room without a jacket!'

An American was motoring through Ireland when he came to a level-crossing, one gate of which was open and the other closed. 'Hey!' he called up to the man in the signal-box, 'why is the crossing only half open?'

'Well, sir,' the signalman shouted back, 'we're half expectin' a train!'

A man on holiday in Spain sent a postcard to his psychiatrist. It read: 'Having a wonderful time. Why?'

The scene: a holiday charter plane bound for the Mediterranean.

Nervous passenger: 'Stewardess, why is this plane jumping and twisting all over the place?'

Stewardess: 'Nothing to worry about, sir. The pilot just took his medicine and he forgot to shake the bottle.'

A holidaymaker was dining in a country inn when he noticed a sign on the wall which read: *Ici on parle Français.*' He said to the manager, 'It's unusual to find an inn in the middle of Cumbria where the staff all speak French.'

'What gave you that idea?' asked the manager.

'Your sign,' said the holidaymaker. 'The one that says "French spoken here".'

'Is that what it says?' exclaimed the manager in surprise. 'I bought it from a young chap who said it meant 'God Bless This House'.

A Scotsman returned home from a holiday in London. That night in the pub he complained bitterly to his friends that his hotel room had cost him £15 a night. 'I'll bet it was worth it, though,' said one of his pals. 'I expect you had a wonderful time sightseeing.'

'I did not!' said the Scotsman. 'I wasn't going to pay that much for a room and not get the proper use of it!'

A young lady on vacation in the country took a walk in the woods one afternoon and came across a large reservoir. It was a lovely sunny day and the water looked so inviting that she stripped off all her clothes and plunged in. At that moment, a policeman appeared on the bank and shouted, 'I've been watching you, miss – there's a law against swimming in this reservoir!'

'Well, why on earth didn't you tell me before I undressed!' shouted the girl indignantly.

'Oh, there's no law against undressing,' said the policeman.

A holiday has been defined as the two weeks when a man stops doing what his boss tells him and starts doing what his wife tells him.

A man went to Italy on holiday and died of wine, women and song. He was serenading a married lady under her balcony and her husband came out and hit him over the head with a bottle of Valpolicella.

An elderly couple arrived in a holiday resort for a week's holiday without having made any hotel reservations. They called in at the resort's top hotel and asked for a room. 'I'm sorry,' said the receptionist, 'but it's the height of the season. We're almost completely booked up – the only thing I could offer you is the Bridal Suite.'

'The Bridal Suite!' exclaimed the old gentleman. 'But we've been married for forty-five years!'

'So what?' said the receptionist. 'If I offered you the ballroom, would you have to dance?'

Tour guides in Europe are certainly keen on tips. They are the only people who can clear their throats in seventeen different languages.

A man was taking his very first holiday cruise and was spending most of the time draped over the ship's rails – probably the first man to cross the Atlantic by rail.

A sympathetic steward who happened to be passing said, 'Cheer up, sir – nobody ever died of seasickness!'

'For God's sake don't say that!' groaned the man. 'It's only the hope of dying that's keeping me alive!'

A Texas millionaire took his wife on vacation to Miami Beach. The wife went down to the beach alone one morning and when her husband strolled down to join her about an hour later he noticed a large crowd at the water's edge. 'Say, what's going on here?' he asked.

'They just pulled some woman out of the water,' said a bystander.

Pushing his way through the crowd, the Texan saw that the woman was his wife. She was lying stretched out on the beach with a lifeguard crouched over her. 'What are you doing to my wife?' the Texan yelled.

'I'm giving her artificial respiration,' said the lifeguard.

'Artificial, hell!' yelled the millionaire. 'Money's no object – give her the real thing!'

It was a strict rule that the staff of the holiday hotel were not allowed to have visitors of the opposite sex in their rooms after ten o'clock at night. A young waitress was entertaining a male guest with whom she had struck up an acquaintance on the first day of his holiday. After a few drinks and some pleasant conversation, she said, 'Well, it's almost ten o'clock – you'll have to get going.'

'OK,' said the young man. 'Turn out the light, then.'

'I hear you went to Puddlesea for your holidays last year. What was it like?'

'Very dreary. In fact it was so dull it didn't even look good in the brochure.'

There's only one book that's really good at helping you decide where to spend your annual vacation – your cheque-book.

'How was Blackpool?'

'Well, we didn't have one rainy day in the whole two weeks.'

'Really?'

'No – we had fourteen.'

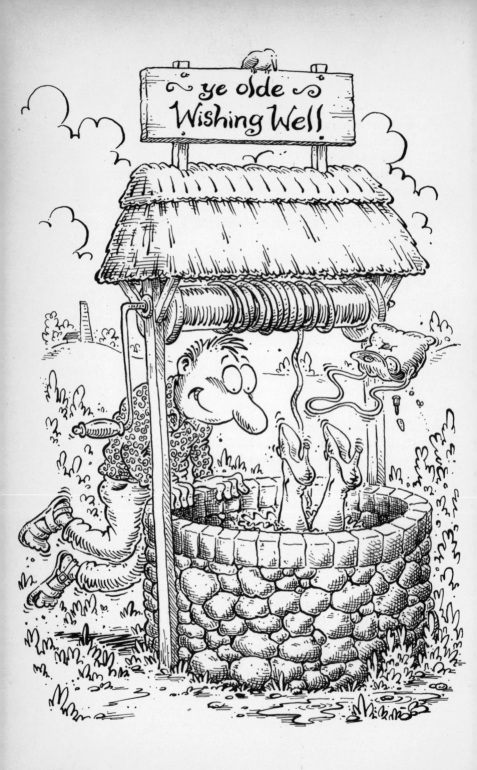

An Irishman on holiday in New York gazed up in awe at the Empire State Building. A conman approached him and said, 'I'm sorry, bud, but we charge a dollar for every storey you look at.'

'Is that right, sorr?' said the Irishman. 'Well, I looked at ten, so here's $10.'

As the conman walked off with the $10 note, the Irishman laughed and said to himself, 'That fooled him! I looked right to the top!'

'How did you enjoy your holiday in Australia?'
'Marvellous! It's got everything for the family – plenty of pubs for me, shops for the wife, beaches for the kids, sharks for the mother-in-law. . . .'

A tourist and his wife in Cornwall were looking with interest at a wishing well, both engrossed in their own private thoughts. The wife leaned over to peer into the depths. Suddenly she overbalanced and fell in.

'Well, I'm blowed!' exclaimed the husband. 'These things really work!'

The holiday charter flight to Majorca had its usual quota of obnoxious small children. One little boy in particular was driving all the passengers crazy by running up and down the aisle, shouting, upsetting drinks and getting in everybody's way. Finally one of the passengers tapped him on the shoulder and said, 'Sonny, would you do me a favour? Go and play outside.'

'I hear you just got back from the South of France?'
'Yes.'
'Did you take the wife along?'
'No – it was a pleasure trip.'

'What was the first thing that struck you in Paris?'
'Well, actually, it was a taxi.'

A consortium of Jewish businessmen have just opened a dude ranch in Arizona. They're calling it the Bar Mitzvah.

For those of you going to Greece for your holidays, the nicest part of the day is 6.30 in the evening. That's the brief moment when the flies have knocked off for the day and the mosquitoes haven't yet come in for the night shift.

First Scotsman: 'And how was London, Sandy?'
Second Scotsman: 'Fine. But awfu' expensive. I was only there a week and £15 went just like that!'
First Scotsman: 'Och, man, that's dreadful!'
Second Scotsman: 'Aye. Next time, I'll go alone.'

A man and his wife were on holiday at the seaside. One morning, they were walking along the promenade when a seagull flew overhead and left its calling card on the wife's new dress. Her husband found this highly amusing, but his wife said angrily, 'Don't stand there laughing your head off! Get some paper!'
'What's the good?' said the husband. 'That bird will be miles away by now!'

'I hear you're not going to Spain this year?'
'No, it's Italy we're not going to this year. It was Spain we didn't go to last year.'

'So your Bert's gone on a package tour to India, has he?'
'Yes, that's right. I had a postcard from him only this morning. Look, here it is.'
'Hmmm. "The Taj Mahal". What's that?'
'I don't know. Must be the hotel he's staying at. What do you think of it?'
'Bit ostentatious. But I do like the swimming pool in front!'

'Where did you go for your holidays?'
'Brighton.'
'What sort of a resort is it?'
'Very friendly. There are lots of girls looking for husbands – and lots of husbands looking for girls.'

Two old ladies were spending a short holiday together in Amsterdam. They wandered round the Rijksmuseum and stopped in front of one picture which bore the title: 'Rembrandt – by himself'. One of the old ladies turned to the other and said, 'Why did they need to put that under the picture? It's quite obvious there's nobody else with him.'

'Haven't seen your wife around lately, old boy.'
'No. She was always going on about getting away somewhere where the sun was always hot and there was plenty of soft sand.'
'Did you fix her up?'
'Yes, I did. It was a bit difficult because they don't usually accept women in the Foreign Legion.'

A passenger heading north for a holiday in the Scottish Borders asked the sleeping car attendant on the London to Glasgow train to wake him at Carlisle. 'I'm a heavy sleeper,' he said, 'and you'll probably have difficulty waking me up. But ignore my protests – just make sure I leave the train at Carlisle.' He retired for the night and woke just as the train was pulling in to Glasgow. He sought out the attendant and shouted angrily, 'I thought I told you to put me off the train at Carlisle! I don't mind telling you I'm very annoyed with you – very annoyed indeed!'

'You're not half as annoyed as the fellow I put off at Carlisle!' said the attendant.

An Irish couple were packing for their annual holiday. As usual, they'd packed too many clothes into their suitcase and were having considerable difficulty in getting it to close.

'Put your weight on it now, Michael,' said the wife.

So Michael wrote, '16½ stone' on the label.

'Did you enjoy your holiday in London, MacTavish?'

'I did that, MacDonald. But they're a funny lot down there, I'll tell ye! All through the night they were banging and hammering on the walls o' my bedroom! Why, I could hardly hear my bagpipes!'

A middle-aged couple had a big win on the pools and decided to take a nice long holiday. 'How about a world cruise?' suggested the travel agent. 'This is a good one. You call in at Valparaiso, Trincomalee, Surabaya, Yokohama, Lourenço Marques. . . .'

'Here, hang on a minute!' said the wife. 'I can't even pronounce half of those places! What's the use of going anywhere if we can't tell people where we've been?'

A young man had just returned from his two-week annual holiday. When he went into work on the Monday morning, he walked into the manager's office and said, 'Sir, could I please have Friday off to get married?'

'But you've just had two weeks off!' said the manager. 'Why didn't you get married then?'

'What!' said the young man. 'And ruin my holiday!'

'And how did you enjoy Paris?'
'Marvellous! We saw everything!'
'Did you see the *Mona Lisa?*'
'If it was in the Louvre, we saw it.'

Two American tourists were visiting London. They went for a stroll one morning, and when they arrived at Buckingham Palace the wife paused to gaze at the great building and watch the Changing of the Guard.

'Let's hurry it up a little!' snapped the husband. 'We're never going to see London if you keep stopping to look at everything!'

A tourist is a man who travels hundreds of miles just to get a photograph of himself standing beside his car.

'I had a wonderful August Bank Holiday,' said the man in the pub to the barman. 'I just sat in a comfortable armchair with a crate of ice-cold beer and watched the reports of 25-mile traffic tailbacks on TV.'

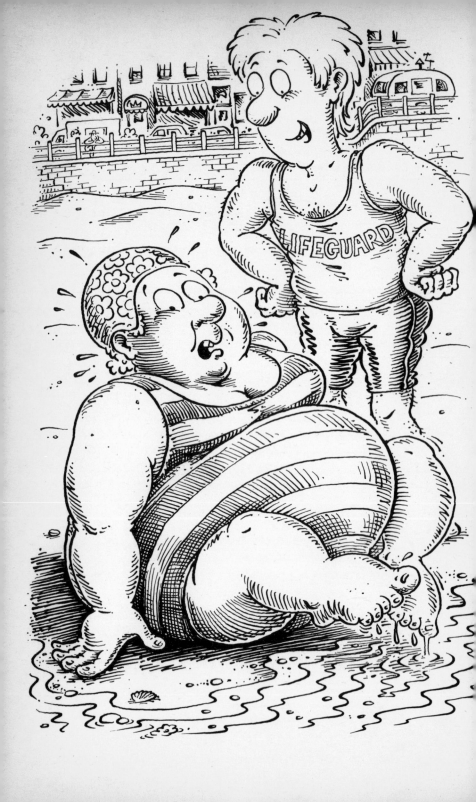

The scene was the boating-pool at a holiday resort. 'Come in, Number 9!' shouted the attendant. 'Your time is up!'

'Hang on,' said his assistant. 'We've only got eight boats!'

'Hello, Number 6!' the attendant shouted again. 'Are you in difficulties?'

Two young fellows were on holiday. Chatting one evening in the bar of their hotel, one of them said, 'I'm going down to the beach tomorrow. Tell me – how do you teach a girl to swim?'

'Well,' said the other, 'you take her into the water, then you put one arm round her waist and, holding her gently but firmly, you lower her into the water. Then you place your right hand delicately under her chin to keep her face out of the water, and let her get used to floating face downwards. Just hold her closely until she gets used to it.'

'Thanks,' said the first fellow. 'I suppose it will take time and patience, but my sister always wanted to learn to swim.'

'Your sister!' exclaimed his friend. 'Oh, in that case, just push her off the end of the pier!'

An extremely fat lady was sunbathing on the beach, when she was approached by a lifeguard.

'Excuse me, madam,' he said, 'but would you mind moving?'

'Why on earth should I?' she asked.

'The tide's waiting to come in,' he explained.

'How come you took your holidays in March?'
'We like to get in early while the sheets are still clean.'

'Did you have any difficulty with your French on the Riviera?'
'No – but the French people did.'

A tourist was standing at the top of a very high cliff in Southern Ireland. He turned to a local farmer and said, 'This is a very dangerous spot. Don't you think there ought to be a notice here warning people to keep away from the edge?'

'Sure,' said the farmer, 'we did have one, sorr, but nobody ever fell over so we took it down.'

Sign in a seaside snack bar: 'Our tongue sandwiches speak for themselves!'

At a dude ranch in South Carolina, one of the holiday guests was attempting to saddle a large horse. 'Pardon me,' said one of the cowboys on the staff, 'but you're putting that saddle on backwards.'

'Oh, yes?' said the holidaymaker. 'And how do you know in which direction I'm going?'

A businessman was returning home from America to Ireland. His daughter was a ground hostess at Shannon Airport, and went out to meet him off his plane. When her father came down the steps, she threw her arms round him and kissed him. An American tourist who was next off the plane dropped his luggage and grabbed her, exclaiming, 'This is what I like about Ireland – their hospitality!'

A man was motoring through Ireland and, finding that he was running short of petrol, pulled up at a small country garage. 'Five gallons, please,' he said to the attendant.

'I'm sorry, Sir,' said the attendent. 'We don't sell petrol here.'

'You don't sell petrol? Then what's the idea of all these pumps and signs?' said the motorist.

'That's just to pull customers in,' replied the attendant, 'so we can give them free air and water.'

'I have a complaint to make,' said a woman to the purser on a holiday cruise. 'A sailor peeked into my cabin last night!'

'Really?' said the purser. 'What do you expect for second class – the captain?'

A tourist was violently seasick on the Cross-Channel ferry from Newhaven to Dieppe. Lying on his bunk, he said weakly to his wife, 'I think I'm going to die. And if I do, dear, please bury me in France. I couldn't stand this trip again, dead or alive!'

Office manager: 'Will you ever forget that marvellous weekend we spent in Paris?'
Secretary: 'How much are you offering?'

A visitor from Yorkshire was spending a week's holiday in London. On his first day, he arrived back at his hotel at eleven o'clock in the evening. 'You're quite late, sir,' said the receptionist.

'Aye, I am,' said the Yorkshireman. 'I've been sightseeing. I got on the tube and there were this sign saying 'Dogs Must Be Carried.' I hunted all over for a dog but I couldn't find one, so I had to walk!'

A Londoner visiting the country was walking across a large field when he found himself confronted by a very fierce-looking bull. 'Is this bull safe?' he called out anxiously to a farmer standing at the gate.

'He's a darned sight safer than you are!' the farmer yelled back.

A man took his wife to Paris for a short holiday. They spent a couple of days together seeing the sights and then, on the third day, the wife went off alone to do some shopping while the husband strolled around Montmartre.

At a pavement café he fell into conversation with a charming Parisienne. All went well until it came to the question of money. She wanted 500 francs. He offered 50. As they couldn't agree, they went their separate ways.

That evening, the man took his wife to a restaurant on the Left Bank. As they walked in, he spotted the young lady he had met earlier in the day, seated at a table near the door. She took one look at the couple as they passed and said loudly, 'You see, *monsieur!* That's what you get for a lousy 50 francs!'

A party of American tourists was being shown round Caernarvon Castle. One of them remarked, 'It sure is a swell place, but why did they have to build it so near the railroad?'

The young holidaymakers had only been married for twelve months. On the second day of their vacation, the wife was rushed to the local maternity hospital. In the waiting room, the anxious husband complained to another expectant father, 'The baby wasn't due for another six weeks! What a thing to happen on holiday!'

'You're lucky,' said the other man. 'I'm on my honeymoon!'

Two married couples went off on holiday together. One evening, in order to make things a little more interesting, they decided to exchange partners. After all, variety is the spice of life!

The next morning, the two husbands met at breakfast. 'Well, I quite enjoyed that,' said the first.

'So did I,' agreed the second. 'I wonder how the girls got on?'

Father climbed out of the car at the crowded family resort on August Bank Holiday Monday and said, 'Well, we finally found a place to park! Does anyone remember why we're here?'

When George returned to the office looking tanned and relaxed, his secretary asked him how he had enjoyed his holiday. 'Well,' he said, 'an old friend of mine asked me to go and stay with him at his cottage in the country. Very secluded, no entertainment, no bars or nightclubs, no girls – miles from anywhere.'

'And did you enjoy it?' asked his secretary.

'I didn't go,' said George. 'I went to Blackpool instead.'

An English couple were visiting the great palace at Versailles. As they strolled through an enormous banqueting room, the husband nudged his wife and said, 'Just look at that couple coming towards us! Typical tourists! Don't they look ridiculous!' When they reached the end of the room, they found that the wall was one enormous mirror.

Two members of the Garda were driving along outside Dublin one evening when they noticed a parked car by the roadside. A man was sitting in the back throwing empty beer bottles out of the window. They pulled up sharply and went across.

'What's the big idea?' said one of the policemen.

'Hello, officer!' said the man cheerfully. 'It's the annual works outing!'

'But you're all by yourself!' protested the other policeman.

'Sure I am!' said the man. 'I'm self-employed!'

O'Halloran had just returned home to Ireland from a three-week walking tour around the Mediterranean.

'How did you get on for drinking water?' asked his pal, O'Casey. 'I hear you can't trust the water in them parts – full of diseases and germs and bacteria.'

'Well, I'll tell you,' said O'Halloran. 'We took great care, so we did. First of all we boiled it, then we strained it and filtered it, and then we boiled it again. And then, just to be absolutely safe, we threw it away and drank Guinness.'

A very busy executive had been persuaded, much against his wishes, to take a trip round the world in a charter plane. Protesting that he had a very heavy workload, with no time to spend on holidays, he boarded the plane, and off they went.

As they were flying over southern Europe, the stewardess, in an attempt to make the trip entertaining, said, 'That's Rome down there, sir.'

'Don't bother me with details,' snapped the executive. 'Just mention the continents!'

There was an interesting item in the papers the other week. It seems the Brighton authorities hired an Eskimo life-guard but they had to let him go because he would insist on giving nose-to-nose resuscitation.

A passenger on a luxury cruise received an invitation to dine at the captain's table. 'Look at this!' he complained to his wife. 'We've paid good money for this cruise and now we're expected to eat with the crew!'

A Scotsman and his wife came south for their holidays. They had always fancied a ride in an aeroplane and were delighted to find that one of the attractions offered by their resort was a 20-minute flight in an old biplane. However, their delight was somewhat tempered when the pilot told them that the charge would be £50 for the two of them.

'Och, that's a lot of money!' complained the Scotsman.

They looked so disappointed that the pilot said, 'I'll tell you what I'll do. I hate being asked questions and pestered while

I'm flying, so if neither of you says a word during the whole trip, I'll only charge you £10.'

Sandy agreed with alacrity and up they went. The pilot gave them the works: dives, spins, stalls, the lot! Half the time they were flying upside down, and when they finally landed the pilot said, 'Well, I've got to hand it to you, sir! It certainly took some courage to go through all that without uttering a single word!'

'Aye,' Sandy agreed, handing over his £10, 'but I don't mind admitting I nearly said something when the wife fell out!'

An English couple on holiday in southern Yugoslavia were advised by the hotel management that there was a strong possibility of a small earthquake in the region. The wife wanted to return home immediately, but her husband calmed her fears. 'There's nothing to worry about, my dear,' he said. 'These things only affect the poorer quarters of the town.'

A keen fisherman took a week's holiday in Southend. Early on the first morning, he walked to the end of the pier and settled down for a day's fishing. A stranger came up and sat down behind him. Hour after hour after hour the stranger sat there, watching intently. By the end of the afternoon, the fisherman could stand it no longer. He turned to the stranger and said, 'Why don't you do some fishing yourself instead of sitting there watching me all day?'

'Oh, I couldn't do that,' said the stranger. 'I haven't the patience for it.'

On the beach at a seaside resort in Cornwall:
'Mummy, can I go in swimming?'
'No, dear – the sea's too rough and dangerous.'
'But Daddy's gone in swimming.'
'Yes, dear, but Daddy's insured.'

The departing holiday guest was waiting in the hotel foyer for his taxi. Suddenly he shouted to the porter, 'Would you run upstairs quickly and see if I left my umbrella in Room 18? It should be in the corner by the window.'

The porter dashed off and arrived back just as the taxi was pulling up outside. 'You're quite right, sir,' he said. 'It's exactly where you said it was!'

'Did you have a good time?' asked Fred's workmates when he came back from holiday.

'No,' he said. 'That resort was so dull, one day the tide went out and never came back.'

A tourist had just returned from a holiday in Arizona. 'It was quite frightening,' he said. 'I was surrounded by Indians! Indians in front of me, Indians behind me, Indians all around me!'

'Good heavens!' said his friend. 'What did you do?'

'What could I do?' said the tourist. 'I bought a blanket!'

Two Irishmen were bound for a holiday in Sardinia. About an hour into the flight, the captain of the charter plane announced that one of the engines was malfunctioning but there was nothing to worry about as they could manage quite easily on the other three. Ten minutes later, he announced that a second engine had cut out; and shortly afterwards, he came through on the intercom again to say that a third engine had packed up.

One of the Irishmen turned to the other and said, 'Do you know what I'm thinking, Mickey? If that last engine goes, we'll be up here all night!'

'We are now passing one of the biggest breweries in Ireland,' announced the guide on a coach trip.

'Why?' protested a voice from the back.

A holidaymaker dashed into a pub on Dartmoor and shouted, 'Somebody help me, quick – my mother-in-law has fallen into a bog on the moors!'

'She'll be all right for a while,' said one of the locals. 'It's not deep – have a pint and then I'll help you pull her out.'

The holidaymaker ordered a beer and some fifteen minutes later, when he had finished it, the local said with a chuckle, 'Right, let's go and rescue your mother-in-law. She's probably in up to her knees by now!'

'Oh, I forgot to mention,' said the holidaymaker. 'She fell in head first.'

A tourist visiting Bournemouth stopped at a hotel for an early evening drink. In the bar he struck up an acquaintance with a very attractive young lady. After a few drinks he took her over to the reception desk and booked a double room for the night, signing in as Mr and Mrs Robinson.

The next morning, after breakfast, he was presented with a bill for £750.

'What's all this?' he exclaimed. 'I've only been here one night!'

'Yes, Mr Robinson,' said the clerk, 'but your wife's been here five weeks.'

An American tourist and his wife returned home from a holiday in Paris, and one evening they were regaling their friends with details of the trip. They had been especially taken by the Louvre, and their favourite picture was a representation of the Temptation of Adam and Eve in the Garden of Eden. 'We found it particularly fascinating,' enthused the wife, 'because, you see, we know the anecdote.'

A couple with a very large and untidy family spent a very pleasant holiday on a farm in Dorset. They decided to go again the following year, and when making the booking the husband said in his letter, 'We thoroughly enjoyed our stay last year except for one little thing, and that was the noise made by all the pigs.'

The farmer replied: 'Don't worry about the pigs, sir. We haven't had any here since you left last year.'

Seaside landlady: 'The only rooms we have at the moment are overlooking the sea. They're £5 a night extra.'
Holidaymaker: 'How much if I promise not to look?'

The walls of the holiday hotel were so thin, you could hear the people in the next room changing their minds. A tired holidaymaker was trying to get to sleep one night when he was disturbed by the honeymoon couple next door. 'Oh George!' said a female voice, 'I can't believe we're really married at last! I can't believe it – I really can't believe it!'

'For God's sake convince her, George,' yelled the holiday-maker. 'I want to get some sleep!'

A couple of American tourists in Paris were dining at an imposing restaurant on the Rue de Rivoli. After waiting for half an hour, the husband finally managed to catch a waiter's eye. 'How long does it take to get served in this dump?' he stormed. 'I want a bottle of your finest champagne!'

'*Mais oui, monsieur*,' said the waiter. 'What year?'

'Right now!' bellowed the American.

I hear you went to Europe for your holidays this year. Which countries did you visit?'

'I don't know. My husband bought the tickets.'

A keen fisherman took a fortnight's holiday at a small hotel near Aberdeen. He caught a large quantity of fish during his stay and generously gave half of his catch to the hotel for the other guests. At the end of his stay, one of the items on his bill read: 'To supplying cooking oil for frying fish: £11.50.'

A charter holiday flight is composed of a group of people with a common interest who get together to hire a plane. For example, there was a charter flight last week which consisted of 120 people who couldn't get on any other charter flight.

A young lady took a luxury cruise to the West Indies. She kept a diary of her holiday and the first week's entries read as follows:

Monday: Captain invited me to dine at his table.

Tuesday: Spent most of the day with the captain.

Wednesday: Captain said he was madly in love with me.

Thursday: Captain said unless he could spend the night with me, he'd scuttle the ship.

Friday: Saved 1000 lives.

'Where did you go for your holidays this year?'
'Spain.'
'Was it your first time in an aeroplane?'
'Yes! I was so scared, I didn't let all my weight down at once!'

Two ragged-looking small boys were paddling at the seaside. 'Ere, ain't your feet dirty!' said one.

'Yeah,' said the other. 'We didn't come on holiday last year.'

An Irishman came over to London for a short vacation at a West End hotel. 'Look here,' he complained to the bell-boy, 'just because I'm from Ireland, don't think you can fob me off with a tiny room like this! Why, its no bigger than a broom closet!'

'Get in, sir, please,' said the bell-boy. 'This is the lift.'

A young lady tourist named Shanker,
Was asleep while the yacht lay at anchor.
She awoke in dismay
When she heard a voice say,
'Just hoist up her top sheet and spanker!'

'Where are you going for your holidays this year?'
'Well, last year we went on a round-the-world cruise, but this year we fancy somewhere different.'

Holidaymaker: 'What's your charge for bed and breakfast?'
Landlady: '£18 or £20 per night.'
Holidaymaker: 'What's the difference?'
Landlady: 'The £20 room has free TV.'

The tourist was chatting to the village's oldest inhabitant outside a country pub. 'And have you lived here all your life?' he asked.
'Not yet,' replied the old man.

A man went into a travel agency and asked where he could go for £25. They told him.

A certain northern town had a splendid old public toilet in the main square. This was looked after by an attendant, an old chap of sixty-five. It came to the attention of the town council that in all the time he had worked for them he had never had a holiday, so arrangements were made for a relief to take his place while he took two weeks off.

When the appointed time came round, one of the councillors was surprised to discover that the attendant had turned up to work as usual, dressed in his best suit. He asked him why he had not gone away.

'Because of your letter,' said the old boy.

'What letter?' asked the councillor.

'The one you sent me telling me that I could have two weeks' holiday at my own convenience.'

An American tourist was visiting a small resort in Yorkshire. Chatting to a local in the village pub, he asked, 'Any big men born in this place?'
'No,' said the local. 'Only babies.'

A Scottish commercial traveller (as they used to call them in the old days) was visiting the Yorkshire Dales, the southernmost part of his territory. It was the middle of winter and heavy snowfalls made all travel impossible, so he sent a telegram to head office in Edinburgh: STRANDED HERE DUE TO BLIZZARDS. PLEASE SEND INSTRUCTIONS.

Back came the reply: START ANNUAL TWO-WEEK HOLIDAY IMMEDIATELY.

A dear little old lady asked a guard at Victoria Station, 'I'm off on my summer holidays – where do I catch my train?'

'All depends on where you're going, Grandma!' said the guard with a smile.

'Mind your own business! And don't be so cheeky!' said the old lady sharply. 'As a matter of fact I'm going to Penzance.'

'Right,' said the guard. 'That's platform 10 – the 12.15 train.' He helped the old lady with her luggage and, after seeing her settled, he got out of the carriage and closed the door.

As the train pulled out of the station, the old lady stuck her head out of the window and called after him, 'Fooled you! I'm not going to Penzance at all – I'm going to Scarborough!'

A family was returning from a holiday abroad. Father had rather more wines and spirits in his luggage than the law allows, and Mother had picked up one or two items that would have been of interest to Customs and Excise. They held their breaths as the customs officer rummaged through their things, and thought they might just get away with it. But then, just at the last moment, their ten-year-old son shouted, 'He's getting warm, Daddy! He's getting warm!'

A vacation is the time of year when you load up the car with half a ton of luggage, the wife and kids, Grandpa and Grandma, two dogs and the budgie – and then tell the neighbours you're going to get away from it all.

The passengers on the holiday flight to the Costa del Sol were just unfastening their seat-belts after take-off when a calm voice came over the loudspeaker and announced, 'Good afternoon, ladies and gentlemen. We are pleased to inform you that this flight is fully automated and runs entirely on computer-controlled instruments. There is no need to worry about a thing as the system has been thoroughly tested and absolutely nothing can go wrong . . . can go wrong . . . can go wrong . . . can go wrong . . .'

A party of Japanese loaded down with cameras was clustered in front of Buckingham Palace to watch the Changing of the Guard. The crowd was so thick that one of them fainted and collapsed in a heap on the pavement. 'Quick!' shouted a tourist. 'Loosen his camera straps!'

Paddy McMahon and his bride Mary decided to spend their honeymoon in London. When they were shown to their hotel room, Paddy looked dejectedly at the twin beds and said, 'I'm sorry about this Mary. I was hoping we'd have a room to ourselves.'

An American on a motoring holiday in Ireland pulled up on a remote country road and shouted to a farmer, 'Hey, Paddy, do you know the way to Killarney?'

'Indeed I do, sir,' said the farmer as he walked away.

Mrs Smythe-Robinson had just returned from a fortnight's holiday on the Continent. She was entertaining her coffee-morning neighbours with a detailed account of her experiences, and to hear her tell it you'd think she had been everywhere and met everyone of any importance.

Her neighbours glanced at each other with cynical smiles, and at last one said sceptically, 'And I suppose you met the Pope?'

'Oh, yes, certainly,' said Mrs Smythe-Robinson. 'A charming man, my dear – simply charming – but *her* I couldn't stand!'

All men are equal, as the old saying has it. And this is certainly true of holidays. The chap who takes a holiday finishes up just as broke as the chap who couldn't afford to.

Michael O'Hara had just returned from a holiday in China. 'Funny place, China,' he told his mates in the saloon bar of the Crown and Anchor. 'They've got some very strange traditions. For instance, in the old days, if a rich merchant was sentenced to be executed, he could pay one of the poor people to take his place. A lot of those poor people made quite a good living by acting as substitutes.'

A young couple were planning to take a motoring holiday along the South Coast. The wife wanted to take her mother with them but the husband was adamant. 'No!' he said firmly. 'Definitely not! She'll ruin the whole trip! You know how she carries on.'

They argued back and forth for several days, and finally the husband gave in and agreed to his mother-in-law coming along. When the wife broke the news to her, the mother-in-law said, 'You're too late! I've already prayed for rain!'

'Where are you going for your holidays this year?'
'Portugal.'
'That's abroad, isn't it?'
'Not if you're Portuguese.'

Two middle-aged holidaymakers had struck up an acquaintance and were sitting on the beach one sunny morning. Suddenly one of them said, 'Just look at that fat woman over there! The one in the red costume. What a repulsive sight! Look, she's waving and smiling in this direction. Do you think she's actually trying to pick me up?'

'I'll ask her if you like,' said his companion. 'She's my wife.'

A young holidaymaker loaded up with luggage tore along the dockside, hurled himself across six feet of water and landed with a tremendous crash on the deck of the Isle of Wight ferry. When he came to, several seconds later, he gasped, 'Wow! I just made it!'

'You needn't have rushed,' said a deckhand. 'This boat's coming in.'

London taxi driver: 'I'm afraid my meter's on the blink, mate, so I'm not sure what to charge you.'
Scots tourist: 'Och, that's all right then – I've no money and I couldn't pay you anyway.'

A visitor to Los Angeles remarked to a local, 'Sure looks like rain today.'
'Rain! said the local. 'Not in California, buddy!'
'But what about those clouds up there?' said the holiday-maker.
'Don't mean a thing, man. They're just empties coming back from Florida.'

An Aberdonian on holiday in London asked the conductor of a bus in Piccadilly, 'What's the fare to Victoria Station?'
'60p,' said the conductor.
Instead of boarding the bus, the Aberdonian ran along behind it for several stops. As it slowed down at a set of traffic lights, he gasped, 'What's the fare to Victoria Station now?'
'90p,' said the conductor. 'You're running the wrong way.'

A young man was taking a short holiday in Paris as the guest of a friend of his who lived there. They were sitting at a pavement café in Montmartre one morning when a beautiful girl walked by.
'That's Françoise,' said the Frenchman. '100 francs.'
Shortly afterwards, another girl walked by and the Frenchman said, 'That's Yvette. 250 francs.'
Ten minutes later a stunning blonde sat down at a nearby table. 'Mimi,' said the Frenchman. '500 francs.'
'Good Lord!' said the Englishman. 'Aren't there any decent, respectable girls in this town?'
'Oh, yes,' replied the Frenchman. 'But you couldn't afford their rates.'

'What time does the train leave for Dover?' asked a holidaymaker bound for the continent.

'10.15 a.m. according to the timetable,' said the guard.

'Hang on!' said the holidaymaker. 'It's 10.35 now. If the train hasn't even gone yet, what's the point of having a timetable in the first place?'

'If we didn't have a timetable,' said the guard, 'how could you tell if the trains were running late?'

The holiday motorist stopped his car at the top of a very steep hill in the Pennines. He noticed a farmer leaning over a gate and said, 'This is rather a dangerous hill, isn't it?'

'Well,' said the farmer, 'it's not dangerous up here, but there's a lot of bad accidents down the bottom.'

Hotel porter knocking on holidaymaker's door: 'Was it six o'clock or seven o'clock you wanted to be called, sir?'

Irate holidaymaker: 'It was eight o'clock, you fool! What time is it now?'

Hotel porter: 'Nine o'clock, sir.'

An old farmer from the West Country was spending a holiday in London with a coach party from his home town. He stopped to buy a newspaper from a stand in Piccadilly Circus. The newspaper-seller looked at the Saturday crowds milling about and remarked, 'Quite a lot of people about today, mate!'

'Oh, ar,' said the old farmer. 'There's a dozen of us up from Puddletown alone!'

An American was taking a round-the-world luxury cruise, and at one of the ports of call he was sitting on the promenade deck watching a group of small native boys diving for coins alongside the ship. 'Say, steward,' he said, 'those young fellers don't seem to be afraid of sharks!'

'No, sir,' said the steward. 'It's their American T-shirts.'

'How's that?' said the American.

'Well, sir,' said the steward, 'they all wear American T-shirts printed with the words "America – the Home of Freedom – the Land of Democracy", and not even the sharks will swallow that!'

When a lady on holiday in America visited an Indian reservation she noticed that one of the Indians was wearing a most unusual necklace. 'What is that necklace made of?' she enquired.

'Alligators' teeth,' said the Indian.

'I suppose that sort of thing is as valuable to you people as a string of pearls is to us,' said the lady.

'Rather more so, actually,' replied the Indian. 'Anybody can open an oyster.'

The only places John likes on the Continent are those in which it's only by an effort of the imagination that you can tell you're not in England.'

W. Somerset Maugham, The Constant Wife

An adventurous couple went on a safari holiday in Africa. They were walking through a jungle clearing when a huge gorilla suddenly leaped out and seized the wife. 'Shoot, shoot!' she yelled to her husband.

'I can't!' he said. 'I've run out of film!'

Holiday cruise passenger: 'How close are we to land, captain?'

Captain: 'Approximately three miles, sir.'

Holiday cruise passenger: 'In which direction?'

Captain: 'Straight down, sir.'

'Which of the Italian cities did your husband like best?'

'Venice.'

'Ah, yes, Venice! All those beautiful canals and bridges and palaces!'

'Oh, he didn't care about those. What he liked about it was that he could sit in the hotel window and fish all day without leaving his room.'

First bus passenger: 'Pardon me, I'm on holiday in London. Where do I get off for the Tate Gallery?'

Second bus passenger: 'Keep your eye on me and get off two stops before I do.'

Two small boys who had never been to the seaside before were taken to Margate for a week's holiday. As they sat on the beach gazing out to sea, one of them said, 'Isn't the ocean big!'

'Yes,' agreed the other. 'And that's just the top of it!'

It was August Bank Holiday Monday at Brighton and the beaches were packed solid. Two seagulls flew over the massed crowds. One of them looked down sadly and said to the other, 'Takes all the skill out of it, doesn't it?'

Two old ladies were taking their first trip abroad. 'Stewardess,' said one 'will you please ask the captain not to travel faster than sound as me and my friend want to talk.'

A fellow went on holiday to Israel and paid a visit to the Sea of Galilee. He saw a sign advertising trips across the lake and asked the boatman how much they cost.

'£25,' said the boatman.

'£25!' exclaimed the tourist. 'That's a bit expensive, isn't it?'

'Well, it is a very famous spot, sir,' said the boatman. 'After all, Our Lord walked across from this very point.'

'At those prices,' said the tourist, 'I'm not surprised he walked!'

On holiday in London, a man took his small son to the zoo. They were standing in front of the lions' cage when the little boy tugged at his father's sleeve and said, 'Daddy, if those lions break loose and eat you up, what bus should I catch to get back to our hotel?'

Some useful hints for holidaymakers: in England, traffic will stop for you if you have a dog on a leash; in France, if you have a beautiful blonde on your arm; in Italy, if you are accompanied by several children; and in Germany if you are wearing military unform.

This build-up in holiday air traffic is really getting worrying. Last month, there were more people over London than in it.

An American was on vacation in England. He paid a visit to a stately home and was particularly struck by the extensive and beautiful gardens. 'Tell me,' he said to the head gardener, 'how do you get lawns as perfect as these?'

'Well, sir,' said the old man, 'first of all, you have to start about four hundred years ago.'

Two small children on holiday in London were visiting the Natural History Museum. They stopped in front of a glass case containing a stuffed kangaroo. 'That's a kangaroo,' the boy explained to his sister. 'It's an extinct creature.'

'Kangaroos aren't extinct,' protested the little girl.

'Well, this one is,' said her brother.

Night was falling and the young holiday couple lay snugly together in their tent on the camping site, surrounded by dozens of other exactly similar ones. 'Isn't it peaceful here, darling?' murmured the young lady. 'Nothing but the sound of crickets!'

'Those aren't crickets, love,' replied the young man. 'Those are zippers.'

Notice outside a disco in Weston-Super-Mare: 'Good clean family entertainment every evening except Thursdays.'

An Englishman on holiday in the south of France booked in at his hotel and was handed a complicated form to fill in. 'Oh, I can't be bothered with this now,' he said. 'I'm very tired and I just want to get my head down. Fill it in for me, will you? My name is on my luggage label.'

The receptionist nodded and carefully wrote at the top of the form: 'Name of guest: Monsieur Genuine Pigskin.'

An English visitor to Paris was standing with his face to a brick wall in a small back street one night when a *gendarme* approached and said, '*Défense de pisser!*'

The Englishman replied, '*Je ne pisse pas, je m'abuse.*'

'*Ah!*' said the gendarme as he walked away. '*Vive le sport!*'

A hiker in Ireland stopped a farmer and asked him how far it was to the nearest town.

'It's ten miles, sorr,' said the farmer. 'But a strong young feller like yourself, sure you'll do it in six.'

Two Irishmen decided to go to Greece for their holidays. As they sat in the plane at Dublin before take-off, they noticed a small red truck alongside pumping fuel into the aircraft. The plane took off and arrived in Paris for a short stopover. Again they saw a little red truck refuelling the aircraft. There was a further stopover at Frankfurt, and sure enough there was a little red truck outside on the tarmac.

One of the Irishmen glanced at his watch and said, 'Won't be long now – we're making very good time.'

'Maybe,' said his friend, 'but that little red truck is beating us to it every time!'

A tourist in Rome noticed a young man in one of the city squares shouting, 'Bananas, lovely bananas, get your bananas here! Only 80p a pound!'

'What's the point of shouting that?' said the tourist. 'They use lire in Italy, and anyway not many Italians understand English.'

'Just the man I've been waiting for!' said the young man with a smile. 'Can you tell me how to get to the railway station?'

A honeymoon couple were staying in an old town in Germany where it was the custom for the nightwatchman to ring a loud handbell every hour on the hour all through the night. 'Darling,' said the young lady, 'why don't we make love every time that bell rings?'

Next morning, the young man staggered from the hotel in a state of complete exhaustion and sought out the nightwatchman. 'Listen,' he said, 'how much would you take to ring that bell every two hours tonight instead of every hour?'

'I can't do that,' said the nightwatchman. 'Last evening, a young lady paid me to ring it every half-hour.'

An elderly lady went to a seaside resort in Cornwall for her holidays. On the beach one morning she watched with interest as the locals prepared to go fishing. 'What are those things on the beach?' she asked one of them.

'Lobster pots,' said the fisherman.

'Good gracious!' exclaimed the old lady. 'Do you mean to say you've trained the lobsters to sit on those things?'

It was the last day of his annual holiday, and as a special treat the guest was served a large piece of gorgonzola cheese at dinner. Now he hated gorgonzola cheese, but he didn't want to offend the hotel staff who had been very kind to him during his stay. So when no one was looking, he removed a plant from its pot on the windowsill, popped the gorgonzola inside and returned the plant to its place. The next morning he returned home.

A week later he received a telegram which read: ALL RIGHT. WE GIVE UP. WHERE DID YOU PUT IT?

Old lady on cruise liner: 'Purser, how often do ships like this one sink?'

Purser: 'Only once, madam.'

'How far is it from here to the Giant's Causeway?' a tourist in Ireland asked the hotel receptionist.

'It's about a twenty-minute walk,' he replied, 'if you run like hell.'

Two American tourists were on a week's vacation in Europe covering nine countries. Halfway through the tour they were having breakfast one morning when one said to the other, 'Say, what country are we in, anyway?'

'What day is it?' asked his companion.

'Wednesday,' replied the other.

'Ah! Then this must be Belgium!'

A young fellow on holiday in Spain was chatting up a local señorita in the hotel bar.

'Do you speak English?' he asked her.

'*Sí*,' she replied, 'a leetle bit.'

'How much?' enquired the young man.

'2000 pesetas,' she said with a smile.

A man said his wife loves holidays but refuses to travel by plane. She claims that the long trip out to the airport makes her car-sick.

Holiday charter flights are so crowded these days! One flight was so crowded last week, the pilot had to go by boat.

Two businessmen were discussing their recent holidays in Europe. 'Did you find much to occupy you in Rome?' asked one.

'Well,' replied the other, 'you know what they say – when in Rome, do what the Romans do.'

'So what *did* you do?' asked his friend.

'I seduced an American schoolteacher,' replied the other.

A husband and wife were asleep on the sands, basking in the sunshine. A small boy walked past on the promenade above them. He was carrying two ice cream cones, and as he passed he stumbled and dropped one of them on to the bare chest of the man below.

'Blimey!' said the man, jumping to his feet. 'That seagull must live in a refrigerator!'

On a train travelling north to Scotland, a holidaymaker said to a fellow passenger, 'This is a long tunnel, isn't it?'
'It's not a tunnel,' said the other. 'It's Manchester.'

A young man booked a fortnight's holiday in Corsica, and on the way he took out an accident insurance policy from a machine in the airport lounge. Next to it was a weighing machine so he popped his money in and stood on the platform. Out came a little card with his weight and a message which read: 'A recent investment will pay high dividends.'

On a cruise holiday to the Caribbean, a man was standing on the promenade deck one afternoon when a fellow passenger appeared carrying a silver hip flask. He walked over to the rails and sprinkled the contents of the flask into the water. Seeing the first passenger watching him, he explained, 'My wife's ashes.'

'You must have loved her very much,' said the first man.

'No,' he replied. 'I hate fish.'

If you think holiday travel is bad now, just imagine what it will be like in the future. You decide to spend two weeks on Mars, but you can't land there owing to thick fog, so they divert you to Saturn and you have to travel the rest of the way by bus.

'How long before we get to Berwick-on-Tweed?' asked the northbound holidaymaker.

'Ten minutes, sir,' said the guard.

'Good,' said the tourist. 'I'm getting off there.'

'That should be interesting,' said the guard. 'I've never seen anyone getting off a train travelling at 85 miles an hour before.'

Holidaymaker: 'What time do you serve meals here?'
Landlady: 'Breakfast from 7 to 10.30, lunch from 12 to 3, tea from 4 to 5, and dinner from 6 to 10.'
Holidaymaker: 'That doesn't leave much time for sightseeing, does it?'

A lady on a luxury cruise went down to the galley and said to the head chef, 'I must congratulate you on your excellent Beef Bourguignon! I wonder if I might have the recipe?'

'Certainly, madam,' said the chef. 'First you take 3000 onions. . . .'

A married couple took their car to Italy for their summer holidays. They stopped at Pisa and parked their car in the shadow of the famous Leaning Tower. An attendant appeared and handed them a ticket for which he collected 10,000 lire. When they returned to their hotel, they told the receptionist about their visit to the Tower and complained about the high parking charge.

'There is no parking charge for visitors to the Leaning Tower,' said the receptionist. 'That was insurance against the Tower falling on your car while it was parked.'

An elderly lady on a sea cruise to Australia stopped the purser on the first day out and said, 'Pardon me, could you tell me where the ladies' toilets are?'

'Port side, madam,' said the purser.

'Oh, dear!' said the old lady. 'I don't think I can wait till then.'

'I hear you took your mother-in-law on holiday with you last year. That must have put a bit of a damper on the proceedings!'

'Not at all. We had a wonderful time playing beach games – burying each other in the sand and so on. That reminds me – I must go back next year and dig her up.'

A young man on a walking holiday in Wales lost his way and stopped at a small roadside cottage. In answer to his knock, an old farmer and his wife appeared at the door.

'Can you tell me how far it is to Llandovery?' he asked.

'Seven miles,' said the farmer.

His wife nudged him and said, 'Better make it three miles, Evan – can't you see how tired the poor fellow is?'

A fellow took a safari holiday in Africa. He was walking through the jungle one day when he noticed a dead elephant with a pygmy standing beside it.

'Who killed this elephant?' he asked.

'I did,' said the pygmy.

'How did you do it?' asked the tourist.

'With a club,' said the pygmy.

'A club?' said the tourist. 'It must have been a very big one.'

'Oh, yes,' said the pygmy. 'There's 250 of us in it.'

A cannibal chief decided to take a holiday, so he booked a cruise on a luxury liner. At dinner on the first night, a steward handed him the menu. 'Never mind that,' said the cannibal. 'Just bring me the passenger list.'

Joe: 'And how did you find the weather in Italy?'
Jim: 'We just went outside the hotel and there it was.'

A holidaymaker was in difficulties in the sea off the end of the pier. 'Help, help!' he shouted. 'I can't swim!'
A drunk on the pier yelled back, 'Well, I can't play the piano but I'm not shouting about it!'

The charter flight bound for the Costa Blanca had completed half of its journey when the captain announced that the plane had developed engine trouble. Things looked serious, and one holidaymaker turned to a vicar sitting next to him and said, 'Go on, Reverend – do something religious.' So the vicar took up a collection.

'Where did you go for your holidays this year?'
'We took the car and drove all over the Continent.'
'Did you enjoy it?'
'I'll say! My wife did all the driving.'
'So you had a chance to admire the scenery?'
'That's right. All I had to do was hold the wheel.'

Eastbourne is a very clean resort. The seagulls even fly upside down.

The seaside boarding house at the small harbour resort was situated right on the sea front. A holidaymaker arriving early one afternoon noticed a large old iron ring next to the front door, so he gave it a pull. The door opened and the landlady appeared.
'That'll be £50,' she announced.
'What on earth for?' said the tourist.
'You've just launched the lifeboat,' she replied.

Here it is, vacation time again. Two weeks devoted to discovering places you should stay away from next year.

The French countryside, seen from a railway carriage, looks strangely unfinished.

Noël Coward

'What are you doing?'
'Packing for my holiday.'
'You're not taking the budgie with you, surely?'
'Yes, I am. And he's a little nervous about it. He's never flown before.'

Have you ever travelled on an El Al charter holiday flight to Israel? They don't have stewardesses. A little old lady comes round with a tray of chicken soup and says, 'Eat, eat – it will do you good!'

Sign seen on Bondi Beach in Australia: 'Girls – please do not bother the lifeguard unless you are actually drowning.'

He: 'How about coming down to the beach with me this afternoon?'
She: 'If I do, will you keep your hands to yourself?'
He: 'Oh, yes.'
She: 'No kissing or cuddling?'
He: 'Certainly not!'
She: 'Then what are we going for?'

Seaside landlady: 'Did you sleep well, sir?'

Holiday guest: 'I didn't sleep a wink all night.'

Seaside landlady: 'I *am* sorry, sir – why was that?'

Holiday guest: 'It was that honeymoon couple in the room next to mine. They were arguing all night about their wedding.'

Seaside landlady: 'Oh dear!'

Holiday guest: 'Yes – they couldn't agree where to have it.'

Two friends decided to take a luxury cruise together. On the third day out, the liner encountered a violent storm and sank hundreds of miles from land. The two friends found themselves alone in an open boat in the middle of the Atlantic. They drifted for days and all seemed lost.

On the morning of the sixth day, one of the men sank to his knees and began to pray out loud. 'Oh, Lord,' he said, 'I know I've been a miserable sinner but if you spare me now, I'll change my ways! I'll go to the church every Sunday, I'll be good to my wife, I'll give up gambling and drinking and chasing women and I'll . . . .'

'Hang on!' said his friend. 'Don't go too far. I think I can see a ship coming.'

A young chap was planning a summer holiday in France. Being a conscientious type he spent three months learning French, and by the time he went over to Paris he was confident that he could make himself understood reasonably easily.

He was walking along the Champs Elysées one morning when a large car pulled up beside him and the driver asked him, in French, the way to the Gare du Nord.

The young man gave detailed instructions, also in French, and was just walking away, very pleased with his proficiency in the language, when he heard the driver say to his passenger in a strong American accent, 'You know, Ellie, that's the first French I've been able to understand since we got here!'

Three drunks loaded down with luggage and obviously off on their holidays arrived at Victoria Station. The train for Dover was just about to leave and it was with the greatest difficulty that the porter managed to get the luggage and two of the men on board. He was too late to help the third man on to the train and it pulled out, leaving him on the platform.

'I'm sorry, sir,' said the porter. 'I wish I could have got you on as well but you left it too late.'

'You're not half as sorry as my mates are going to be,' said the drunk. 'They came to see me off.'

A little boy on the promenade at Margate was banging his bucket and spade against the sides of a gleaming new white Porsche parked at the roadside. 'Stop that at once!' yelled his mother. 'I've told you before – if you break that bucket and spade, you won't get another!'

She was only going away for the weekend but she had packed four suitcases, a trunk, a hamper and twelve carrier bags. The only thing she left behind was a note for the milkman.

An old lady on her annual vacation was travelling on a north-bound train. She asked the guard to tell her when the train reached Doncaster. The guard was so busy that he completely forgot, and it was only when the train was pulling out of Doncaster that he remembered the old lady's request. He immediately advised the driver on his internal phone, and the driver stopped the train and reversed back into Doncaster station.

'Here you are, madam,' said the guard. 'This is Doncaster. Let me help you with your luggage.'

'Oh, I'm not getting off here,' said the old lady. 'You see, I don't have a wrist-watch and my daughter told me that when we reached Doncaster, it would be time to take my pills.'

A friend of mine takes several holidays every year. He winters in Switzerland, summers in France, and springs at blondes.

The wife was very keen on a holiday in Russia. The husband had his doubts but finally gave in and booked a fortnight in Moscow. When they were alone in their hotel room, he looked around and whispered cautiously, 'These places are bugged, you know. We'd better take a look around.' Sure enough, under the bed he found some strange-looking wires. Using his pocket knife, he managed to saw through them, and they went to bed feeling a little more at ease.

The next morning at breakfast, the waiter said, 'A very strange thing happened last night, sir! The chandelier in the foyer suddenly fell down!'

An English tourist was travelling home by train from Switzerland. As the train neared the German border, he grew very nervous, and at length he confided to the other occupant of the compartment, 'I bought this watch in Switzerland and I'm going to smuggle it through customs.' At that moment, the customs officer walked into the compartment and asked if they had anything to declare.

'No, nothing,' said the man with the wrist-watch.

At which the second man said, 'What about that new wrist-watch you bought in Switzerland?'

The customs officer promptly confiscated the watch and gave the man a stern lecture on smuggling.

When he had gone, the Englishman turned to his companion and said, 'Thank you very much! I suppose you enjoy getting people into trouble like that?'

'Not at all,' said his companion with a smile, as he pulled a suitcase from under the seat. He unlocked it and there inside were over a hundred brand-new, expensive Swiss watches. 'There you are,' he said. 'Help yourself to a couple of those!'

A French girl came over to the north of England for a holiday and had the misfortune to lose all her money. She had no way of getting back to France and was in despair until she met a kindly sailor who told her that his ship was sailing that very evening and he would smuggle her aboard and make her comfortable down in the hold with a mattress, blankets and food. All he required in return was a little *amour*.

The French girl agreed reluctantly, and that night the sailor smuggled her on board his ship. Twice a day, the sailor visited the girl carrying a tray of food, and twice a day he got his reward.

The days turned into weeks, and this might have gone on indefinitely if the captain hadn't noticed the sailor's twice-daily visits to the hold. He went down to see what was going

on, discovered the French girl and heard the whole story. 'A clever plan,' he said at last. 'Very clever! However, I feel I ought to tell you, miss, that this happens to be the Liverpool to Birkenhead ferry.'

Landlady at seaside boarding-house: 'We like it quiet here. You haven't brought a transistor radio, have you?'
Holiday guest: 'No.'
Landlady: 'And are the children noisy?'
Holiday guest: 'No, they're very quiet.'
Landlady: 'What about that dog – does he bark?'
Holiday guest: 'Never makes a sound. But there is one thing I feel perhaps I ought to mention.'
Landlady: 'What's that?'
Holiday guest: 'I have a fountain pen that scratches a little.'

It was an El Al holiday charter flight to Tel Aviv. As the passengers settled into their seats, the voice of the chief stewardess came over the intercom: 'Good afternoon, ladies and gentlemen, and welcome aboard. I am your chief stewardess, Mrs Miriam Feinberg, and your other hostesses are Mrs Dora Cohen and Mrs Maureen Abrahams. And then, of course, there's my son, the pilot . . . .'

Wife to seasick husband on holiday cruise: 'Cheer up, dear – at least you're beginning to look like your passport photo!'

A young couple returned from a two-week holiday on the Continent. Pinned to their front door was a note from their neighbours. It read: 'We've left you a welcome-home present by the back door-step!' When they looked round the back, they found another note, this time from the milkman. This one read: 'Thanks a lot for the bottle of Scotch!'

The following entry recently appeared in a holiday guide-book: 'Albion Hotel: Bed, Breakfast and Evening Male £25 per night.'

Thanks to modern jet travel, holidaymakers can fly from London to Paris in one hour. That's nothing – history tells us that Helen of Troy got to Paris in ten minutes!

Two Irishmen were taking a late holiday in Scotland. On the first night there was a violent rainstorm, and the next morning at breakfast one of them said, 'Did you hear that rain last night? Wasn't it terrible? And the noise that thunder made!'
'Now why didn't you wake me?' said his friend. 'You know I can't sleep through a thunderstorm!'

A man was telling his mates in the pub about driving to Greece for his holidays. 'It took me six days – four days to drive there and two days to refold the maps!'

A lady tourist posed for a photograph near her car in front of the ruins of an ancient temple in Athens. 'Better not get the car in the picture,' she said to her friend with the camera. 'I don't want my husband to think I ran into the place.'

A tourist was driving his Rolls-Royce on a holiday trip through Switzerland. Negotiating a tricky mountain pass one day, one of the car's rear springs broke. He managed to make it to the nearest town and got in touch with the Rolls-Royce representative in Basle. Within hours, a mechanic travelled out and replaced the spring. The tourist returned home without further mishap.

Some months later he realized that he hadn't received a bill for the repair work, so he wrote to the Rolls-Royce office in London asking them to bill him for the replacement of the broken spring. The reply arrived three days later. It read: 'Dear sir, There is no such thing as a broken spring on a Rolls-Royce.'

A man decided to spend his summer holidays in a remote part of North Wales. He wrote to the proprietor of a small hotel and received the following letter in reply: 'I should like to know, please, whether you want two bedrooms with double beds in them, or two double-bedded rooms, as I have only one double-bedded room; all the beds are double beds except one in the double-bedded room, which is a single bed.'

First holidaymaker: 'Isn't the weather here absolutely awful!'
Second holidaymaker: 'Yes, but it's better than nothing.'

A man and a woman walked into a travel agency, where the booking clerk told them that they were the millionth customers the firm had had since it opened. In honour of the occasion, they were offered a free luxury cruise around the Mediterranean.

On their return, the lady called in at the agency to tell them how much she had enjoyed the holiday. 'I'm so glad it was to your liking,' said the booking clerk. 'There's only one thing that puzzles me,' said the lady. 'Who was that charming gentleman I had to share a cabin with?'

An old lady from Edinburgh on her first visit to London was persuaded to pay a visit to the zoo. She provided herself with several large packets of peanuts and headed for the monkey cage; but to her disappointment, there was not a monkey to be seen. She mentioned this to a keeper who said, 'Well, you see, madam, it's the mating season. They're all round the back. You know – making love.'

'Do you think they'd come out for peanuts?' asked the old lady.

'Would you?' replied the keeper.

A Glasgow man returned from a holiday in London and was asked how he had got on. 'Fine!' he said. 'It's a bonny place and nae mistake! The only trouble was they couldna understand my accent.'

'Accent?' said his friend. 'I've known you for years, Donald, and I didna ken you had an accent!'

A tourist arrived at a small hotel in a remote part of Wales and on unpacking his bags, discovered that he had forgotten to bring his shaving kit with him.

'Oh, don't worry about that, sir,' said the old porter. 'There's a fellow in the village who does a lot of shaving around here. I'll fetch him for you.'

He returned to the hotel some ten minutes later accompanied by a man even older than himself, who unpacked his shaving gear and then insisted that the tourist lie flat on his back.

Somewhat puzzled, the tourist complied, and when the shaving had been completed, he asked the old man, 'Tell me, why did I have to lie on my back?'

'Well, sir,' the man replied, 'I always shave them in that position. As a matter of fact, you're the first living man I've ever shaved.'

'We did so much sightseeing on holiday last year that by the end of the first week our eyes were sore!'

'Then what happened?'

'Then they showed us the sights for sore eyes!'

Two anglers took a fishing holiday in the West Country. One day they were fishing on a private river in a large country estate when the head gamekeeper suddenly appeared. Immediately one of the fishermen dropped his rod and took to his heels, hotly pursued by the gamekeeper. Five minutes later, the gamekeeper caught up with him and grabbed him by the arm.

'Don't you know this is a private river?' he shouted. 'You need a permit to fish here.'

'I've got a permit,' said the angler. 'Here it is.'

He produced the necessary authorization from his pocket.

The gamekeper examined it closely and said, 'Why on earth did you run away if you've got a permit?'

'Well,' said the angler, 'my mate hasn't got one, so I had to give him time to get away.'

A holidaymaker who had returned from a very unpleasant two-week vacation at a seedy hotel in Italy wrote to the package operator to complain that his room had been infested with bugs. A week later he received a reply, offering their deepest apologies and stating that they had never had a complaint of this nature before and were taking immediate steps to ensure that such a thing never happened again.

However, the holidaymaker's original letter had been enclosed in the envelope by mistake. Across the bottom, someone had scribbled, 'Send this idiot the usual bug letter.'

A tourist in Cairo was being pestered by an Arab trader who was trying to sell him a filthy old carpet.

'Lovely carpet, mister – very cheap!' said the Arab.

'No, thank you!' said the tourist in disgust. 'This carpet stinks!'

'No, no!' cried the Arab. 'Carpet no stink! That's me!'

Two Englishmen on holiday on the Isle of Capri were watching a particularly beautiful sunset. After a long pause, one said to the other, 'Not bad, eh?'

'No,' admitted the other. 'But there's no need to go raving mad about it, old boy.'

'How did you enjoy your holiday in Venice?'
'When we arrived, we found that all the streets were under water and everyone had to get about in boats, so we came straight home again.'

'We don't have a single room left in the hotel, sir,' said the receptionist to the holidaymaker who had arrived without a reservation. 'Unless you're prepared to share with a red-headed schoolteacher.'

'How dare you!' said the visitor. 'I happen to be a respectable married man!'

'That's all right, sir,' said the receptionist. 'So is he.'

The airport arrival lounge was packed with returning holidaymakers when suddenly an announcement came over the loudspeaker system: 'Will the lady who left her hearing aid on incoming Flight 145 from Dublin please call at the Aer Lingus Information Desk.'

A tourist on a motoring holiday in the West Country was driving along one sunny morning when he spotted a very attractive young lady trying to hitch a lift. Naturally he stopped and picked her up, and they chatted pleasantly for the first ten minutes or so. Then he asked her what she did for a living and she said, 'Actually, I'm a witch.'

The man laughed and said, 'I thought there was no such thing as witches!'

Whereupon the young lady threw her arms around his neck and he turned into a lay-by.

Three Scotsmen on holiday in New York were staying at a new 45-storey hotel. They returned late one night after an evening on the town to be greeted by the night clerk who informed them that, due to a mechanical fault, the elevators were out of action and they would have to walk up to their room. As this was situated on the 45th floor, you can imagine their feelings.

However, they put a brave face on it. They decided that they wouldn't bother to carry their heavy overcoats all the way up, so they left them with the night clerk.

'Now lads,' said Donald as they set off, 'we've a long way to go, so I suggest that for the first fifteen floors, I tell stories to while away the time. Sandy, you take over for the next fifteen floors, and Tammy, you do the last fifteen.'

All went well for the first thirty floors, and when they arrived at the 31st Donald said, 'Now Tammy, it's your turn for a tale.'

'And a sad tale it is, too!' said Tammy. 'I've left the keys in my overcoat pocket!'

A tourist was driving along a country road in Somerset when he saw a tractor with two men on it turning slowly out of a gate ahead of him. There was no time to pull up so he yanked the wheel hard over, crashed through the hedge next to the gate and careered into the field from which the tractor had just emerged. He bumped across the field until he came to a gap in the hedge further on, and turned through it on to the road again. One of the men on the tractor turned to the other and said, 'You know, Bert, I reckon we just got out of that field in time!'

A Londoner was motoring to Scotland for his annual holiday. He stopped at a fork in the road and asked a local farmer whether the right-hand road led to Carlisle. 'I don't know, sir,' said the farmer. Deciding to take a chance, the motorist set off down the right-hand road. He had proceeded about a hundred yards when he caught sight of the farmer in his rear-view mirror. The man had been joined by a second farmer and was gesticulating wildly. Slowly and carefully the motorist reversed down the road until he drew level with the two men.

'This is my mate,' said the farmer. 'I've asked him and he don't know neither!'

One luxury cruise is so expensive, it costs you £750 to be a stowaway.

Thanks to the speed of modern jet travel, holidaymakers can now be sick in countries they have never even heard of before.

'Would you like to see where I got sunburned?' said the young lady coyly to her boyfriend.

'Yes, please!' he said eagerly. So she showed him a picture of Brighton beach.

A holidaymaker in Ireland noticed this sign at the roadside by a fast-flowing river: FLOOD NOTICE. WHEN YOU CAN'T SEE THIS SIGN, THE RIVER IS UNDER WATER.

A customs officer was examining the luggage of returning holidaymakers at Heathrow. He opened the suitcase of an attractive young lady and inside he discovered seven pairs of new silk panties bearing a Paris label. 'Why seven pairs?' he asked her.

'One for each day of the week,' she said. 'Monday, Tuesday, Wednesday . . . .'

'All right,' said the customs officer, and turned his attention to a battered old suitcase belonging to a very stout middle-aged woman. Inside he found twelve pairs of outsize bloomers.

Before he could ask the obvious question, the woman said, 'January, February, March, April . . . .'

A vicar on a train just about to depart watched a man get on and lean out of the window to talk to his friend on the platform.

'Thanks for a wonderful holiday, George,' he said. 'It was good of you to put me up.'

'My pleasure,' said his friend. 'The food was excellent,' said the man on the train. 'And your wife was great. I really enjoyed sleeping with her.'

When the train pulled out, the vicar couldn't contain himself and he said to the man, 'I know it's none of my business, but did I understand you to say you had enjoyed sleeping with your friend's wife?'

The man smiled sheepishly and said, 'Well, to tell you the truth, I didn't enjoy it at all, but George is a good friend of mine and I didn't want to offend him.'

A tourist in Zimbabwe was sitting in the hotel bar one evening when in walked a tiny man only six inches tall. He was smartly dressed in a tweed jacket, corduroy trousers and suede shoes, and the barman lifted him carefully on to a bar-stool and said, 'Good evening, Major. The usual?'

The tiny figure nodded and the barman served him with a pink gin. The tourist gazed in amazement and then called the barman over and asked who the little military man was.

'Oh, that's Major Danvers,' said the barman. 'He's a very interesting man. I'll introduce you if you like . . .Major Danvers, there's someone here who'd like to meet you. Tell him about the time you told that witch doctor to go and jump in the lake.'

A tourist was motoring through the Lake District. Passing through a small village, he saw a young man running hard with three large, ferocious-looking dogs close behind him. The tourist pulled up, threw open the car door and shouted, 'Get in quick!'

'Thanks a lot,' said the young man. 'Most people won't offer me a lift when they see I have three dogs!'

A Catholic priest was feeling under the weather and his doctor advised a change and a rest. The priest took a few weeks off and went up to London. He soon began to enjoy himself and, after seeing all the sights, he decided he'd like to sample the bright lights of the West End. He became so carried away that, on passing a striptease club in Soho, he resolved to throw caution to the winds and see what it was like.

He was soon thoroughly enjoying himself and he particularly admired one of the strippers, a young lady with a stunning

figure. After her act was over, she came across to his table and said, 'How did you like the show, Father O'Hara?'

'How in heaven did you you know my name?' gasped the priest. 'If the bishop finds out about this, I shall be defrocked!'

'Oh, don't worry about that,' said the stripper. 'Don't you recognize me? I'm Sister Mary – we have the same doctor.'

On the very day that Mickey Malone got back to Ireland from his holiday in Spain, he dropped dead. At the wake, his friend O'Reilly said to the widow, 'He looks very well, doesn't he? What a wonderful tan!'

'Yes,' agreed Mrs Malone. 'That fortnight in Spain did him the world of good.'

'And he looks so happy,' said O'Reilly.

'Yes, well, he died in his sleep, you see,' said Mrs Malone. 'When he wakes up in the morning and finds he's dead, the shock will kill him!'

An Englishwoman returning from a Mediterranean holiday was travelling through France by train. She decided to have a meal in the restaurant car and left her valuable fur coat in the care of a Frenchwoman in the compartment. When she returned, the Frenchwoman was wearing the coat and refused to give it up. The English lady called the guard, but the Frenchwoman stubbornly maintained that the coat was hers. When the train reached Paris, the two women were detained and the railway authorities contacted the British Consul.

When this gentleman arrived, he took the coat away to examine it. On his return a few minutes later, he said, 'This is a very serious matter. I have just discovered a packet of heroin sewn into the lining of this coat.'

The Frenchwoman immediately confessed that the coat was not hers, and hurriedly departed.

Seeing the worried look on the English lady's face, the Consul said, 'No need to be concerned, madam. There is nothing in the coat. I just wanted to find out who it really belonged to.'

A tourist motoring through the West Country stopped a local farmer and asked, 'Am I on the right road for Tiverton?'

'Don't know,' said the farmer.

'Well,' said the motorist, 'can you tell me how to get to Gloucester?'

'No idea,' said the farmer.

'How far is it to Hereford, then?' said the motorist.

'Can't tell you,' replied the farmer.

'You don't know anything, do you?' said the tourist.

'I know one thing,' said the farmer. 'I ain't lost like you!'

A holidaymaker on a walking tour of East Anglia was trying to get a room for the night at a small hotel.

'I'm afraid we have nothing at all,' said the receptionist.

'It's only for one night,' said the tourist. 'Are you sure you can't squeeze me in?'

'Well we do have one permanent resident, an old gentleman called Mr Harrington. There's an extra bed in his room, and he won't mind if you use that as long as you don't disturb him in the morning.'

'That's fine,' said the tourist. 'Perhaps you'd give me a call at seven o'clock.'

Next morning he received his call, dressed quietly and went down to pay his bill. 'Good morning, Mr Harrington,' said the receptionist.

Somewhat surprised, he paid his bill and, as the reception clerk said, 'Sorry you're leaving us, Mr Harrington,' he hurried out of the hotel.

'Morning, Mr Harrington,' said the doorman as he passed.

Even more bewildered, he walked across to the taxi rank and said to the driver of the first cab, 'To the station, please.'

'Certainly, Mr Harrington,' said the cab driver.

By this time the tourist was begining to get panicky. At the station he hurried into the washroom, and for the first time that day caught sight of his reflection in the mirror. 'Oh, my God!' he gasped. 'They woke up the wrong man!'

A rather pedantic old professor was taking an autumn holiday in Ireland. He had planned a day trip to Killarney and he asked at the railway station what time the next train departed.

'10.15, sir,' said the booking clerk.

'Be specific, man!' the professor snapped. 'Is that Greenwich Mean Time, Double Summer Time, British time, Irish time, or what?'

'Sure,' said the booking clerk, 'that's just God's good time.'

On a tour of villages and country towns in Devon, a visitor stopped at a local pub for a drink. Chatting to the barman, he pointed to a row of grizzled old men sitting outside on the village green and said, 'Who's the oldest inhabitant in this place?'

'We haven't got one, sir,' said the barman. 'He died last week.'

A family from Birmingham spent a fortnight in one of those holiday camps last summer. Actually, they were only there for seven days. They got a week off for good behaviour.

'Is Bournemouth really a good place for rheumatism?'
'Oh, yes. That's where I got mine.'

A drunken tourist staggered up to a policeman in London and said, 'Offisher – where am I?'

'Corner of Oxford Street and Park Lane, sir,' said the policeman.

'Never mind the details,' said the drunk. 'What town am I in?'

O'Halloran had driven up to Dublin for a short holiday. Being unused to city traffic, he took a corner on the wrong side of the road and ran smack into another car coming in the opposite direction. He staggered over and discovered to his horror that the other driver was a priest.

'Are you all right, Father?' he gasped. 'This is terrible! I'm so sorry – here, have some whisky – take a swig of this to calm your nerves.' He pulled a hip flask from his pocket and handed it to the priest, who accepted it gratefully and took a long drink.

'You really should be more careful,' said the priest at last. 'You could have killed me!'

'My fault entirely,' said O'Halloran. 'Have another drink to steady your nerves.'

The priest took several more swigs of whisky and then said, 'Aren't you going to have a drink?'

'No, Father, I'm all right, thank you,' said O'Halloran. 'I'll just sit in my car and wait until the police arrive.'

Jane: 'You remember that holiday we had last year in Spain?'
   Sue: 'Yes.'
Jane: 'And you remember that Spanish waiter I was going out with?'
   Sue: 'Which one?'
Jane: 'The one I said I couldn't live without.'
   Sue: 'Oh, that one! What about him?'
Jane: 'I've forgotten his name.'

An Irishman phoned a travel agency and asked, 'How long does it take to fly to London?'
   Turning to his timetable, the clerk said, 'Just a minute, sir.'
   'Thanks very much,' said the Irishman, and hung up.

A young lady was going off on holiday alone to the South of France. 'Now you be careful,' said her mother. 'I don't really like you going off on your own like this. Don't do anything that would make me worry about you.'
   At the end of the first day of her holiday, the young lady met a very attractive lifeguard who invited her out to dinner. Afterwards they went for a stroll and the young man tried to put his arms around her.
   'Don't do that!' she said. 'My mother would worry!'
   Then he tried to kiss her and again she said, 'Don't do that! My mother would worry!'
   Then he asked her if he could come up to her room.
   'Oh, no!' she said. 'My mother would . . . oh, what the hell! . . . we'll go up to *your* room – let *your* mother worry!'

A visitor to London was being shown round the city by a tourist guide. The guide stopped in front of a glass-walled monstrosity of a skyscraper and said proudly, 'This is the latest addition to our architectural heritage! Fifty storeys high, constructed entirely of glass, steel and concrete! And it's completely indestructible by fire!'

'What a pity!' murmured the tourist.

Two Dubliners took a day trip into the country and enjoyed themselves so much that they missed the last bus home. They had consumed quite a few pints of Guinness by this time, so they decided to go down to the bus station and steal a bus. One of them broke into the bus depot while the other one waited outside.

He waited for about half an hour, while from inside the depot there emerged a series of deafening bangs and crashes. At last his friend came out at the wheel of a bus. 'Sorry about that,' he explained. 'The Dublin bus was at the back!'